RED OLEANDERS

A drama in one act

RED OLEANDERS

A drama in one act
By

Rabindranath Tagore

Translated into English by the Author

NIYOGI
BOOKS

Published by
NIYOGI BOOKS
Block D, Building No. 77,
Okhla Industrial Area, Phase-I,
New Delhi-110 020, INDIA
Tel: 91-11-26816301, 26818960
Email: niyogibooks@gmail.com
Website: www.niyogibooksindia.com

ISBN: 978-93-81523-21-6
Publication: 2012
First reprint: 2019

Cover Design: Global Publishing Solutions, Noida
Printed at: Niyogi Offset Pvt. Ltd., New Delhi, India

Red Oleanders
An Interpretation

FOR THOSE of us who are concerned with life and with the play of human forces across the stage of our daily existence, it is the underlying significance which forms the kernel of the problem. In this play there is no attempt to point a moral or to preach a sermon, but because these characters "are the abstract and brief chronicles of the time," they give us a mirror in which perhaps we may catch some glimpse of that truth to which we are so accustomed

---

1   *The interpretation by Tagore himself was published in the Visva-Bharati Quarterly, November 1951-January 1952, with a note: Notes on a talk given by Rabindranath Tagore and transcribed by Leonard K. Elmhirst during the Poet's visit and stay in Argentina, November-December 1924. Reprinted in Rabindra-Racanabali, vol. 16, by West Bengal Government.*

that we have forgotten all about it. The test of every great work of art, in colour, sound, form or word, is this test of significance. The artist has had something great to say and he has said it greatly, so truth is revealed. But to do this, and much modern work shows a woeful lack of consciousness in the matter, life itself must be a great work of art, so that out of the significance of his life a man will draw forth that which holds the essence of truth, and, with the tool over which he has the most complete mastery, will give to it artistic shape. There are those who, in perfecting their tool of craftsmanship, spend their whole lives comparing their facility of use with that of others and await with anxiety the plaudits or criticisms of their fellow craftsmen. This is not so with him who lives greatly. Out of the wealth of his experience of life and of his conviction of truth he draws that which is most truly significant and offers it to us chiselled with no doubting hand and illuminated by his own creative imagination.

In daring to sit in judgement upon _Red Oleanders_, we are not judges, we are the accused. For we stand in front of a great life, the life of one who has lived and drunk of the draft of life from foam to dregs, so that according to our judgement we shall stand judged. The figure on the canvas cannot be separated from its background, else the unity of truth is broken. The background to this play is one which needs careful attention if the characters, as they step upon the stage, are to tell their tale, and keep their significance. Divest them of this and it is so easy to be superficial, to repeat the catchwords of the modern market place; a poetic tirade against modern industrialism, the usual hit at Science, the national complaint of the subject against oppression. But whether we will or no, the forces that we ordinarily applaud are beaten at the end. They dissolve before the close into a complete insignificance and vanish in the face of a superior force which somehow convinces us, whether we see its significance or not.

In *Red Oleanders*, there are certain underlying principles at work, principles which we can quite easily recognize in our own daily existence if we choose to look for one moment under the surface. The habit of greed—greed for things, for power, for facts, with all the ramifications that greed is able to set up between man and man—is arrayed against the explosive force of human sympathy, of neighbourliness, of fellowship and of love, the force which we may term good. Good is here arrayed against the dehumanizing force of mammon, of selfishness, of evil; of that which separates us from our fellows against that which cements us together, of that which because it divides us, is untruth, is a lie. Only in so far as he recognizes this truth, has man succeeded in reaching the peak upon which the human race now stands, whilst the tiger, a solitary wandering unit, still prowls the jungle alone.

To the gardener of a northern clime the oleander is a flowering shrub, which, because of the character of its foliage and the simple beauty of its red blossoms, well repays careful attention and its place inside the heated greenhouse. In more temperate regions the oleander finds its welcome in the open garden, and will lavish its splendour within the courts of palace or monastery, whilst in India it flourishes of its own accord over jungle and plain. It has the same flower, the same nature, the same principle of growth, but according to temperature and environment it finds devotion from one, appreciation from another, and only cursing and bitterness from the poor cultivator, who, as its roots spread from the hedgerow and invade his scanty plot, must set to work with his *kodali* and root it out. In his struggle for livelihood he is concerned with the underground ramifications of the root system, and with his eyes upon the soil he lacks either the time or the energy to glance as the spray of red blossoms that hangs immediately over his head.

Into a world where men have sacrificed every simple human relationship and are grubbing for what they can get, out of each other, out of the soil, out of books or the exploitation of souls, where the beauty of human sympathy is forgotten, the oleander sheds its flower, and, with a shock, some with protest, some in anger, some in response to a deep echo within, cast away their tools and according to their several abilities realize that beauty of life which had dwelt among them, but which they had allowed to grow out of reach.

The background, then, is a world based upon the principle that each must fight the other, oppress or be oppressed, in order not merely that the ordinary simple needs of life may be satisfied, but that piles of accumulation may be set up. This is a world where, with every available means in his power, the Great King exploits the resources of the underworld, of nature, of the mind, of science and of human physique and intelligence, using all the weapons of organization and the elaborate machinery of a highly centralized bureaucracy in order to add to his wealth. This wealth he measures in gold, or in souls or in facts, or in human bodies, so that men are men no longer but numbers. The King sits fascinated as he watches this hive where everyone is busy, but no one content, where all are piling cell to cell, adding honey to honey, guarding the stores of accumulated wealth with efficient death-dealing stings, or casting out the human wastage, the drones, men who have been broken, or exploited. Into his hive flies the butterfly, armed with no sting, equipped with no power to gather or to store, but clothed in beauty, loving the light of day and life, asking all to share in her sunshine revels, kissing one here and one there with the waft of her wings, arousing a petulant anger where others are too busy even to look at her and are annoyed when she interferes with the work in hand. Like strings on an untuned instrument they respond to her touch, and though the instrument had long been thrown on one side, still here and there music and harmony come struggling forth, toils and troubles are forgotten, memories are aroused of the old scents and sounds, of the simple artistic colour and variety of nature, of the co-operative life of her village, where all were not numbers but neighbours, where there was music and beauty and life. But we have become numbers, with numbers on our doors, our telephones, our cars, our factories, our restaurants, our votes, and our tickets at sports or theatre. Even as worshippers we are card indexed.

Nandini then is this touch of life, the spirit of joy in life. Matched with Ranjan the spirit of joy in work, together they embody the spirit of love; love in union, union in love, a harmony before which the discord of greed is scattered as under a spell. Linked in his harmony of beauty they walk fearlessly into this world of getting, and being independent of it, they break down its barriers. even though in the process they are broken themselves,— but such sacrifice is the price which must always be paid in the effort to break down the wall of the darkness, of untruth and to flood the world with light. In the face of this combination of simplicity, the king, enclosed in his pride of empire, in his accumulation of wealth, of things, finds a touch of that happiness that he had lost. His gold loses its lustre, his scientific experiments, involving the crushing out of human life, and with it of faith and hope, no longer give him interest. His research into elemental forces, which in his curiosity he has broken down from compounds to molecules, from molecules to atoms, is dazzled and confounded by the beams of a beauty that warms and embraces everything under its cloak of human affection and sympathy.

So it is that, when men make use of men and leave out this elemental touch of kindliness, by which alone we may live in harmony with our surroundings, they crush and mutilate not merely their victims but the humanity which is in themselves. They prefer to think in terms of empire, of organization in factory or field or workshop, in politics or church or sport, and to satisfy their craving for power or survival at the expense of their human feelings. They use every variety of machinery to fortify themselves or their selfish ends against the dissolving power of beauty and love,—the trust, the company, stocks and shares, investments, machinery through which they can avoid all human connection and so cut themselves off from their fellows whilst they extract for their own benefit the very essence of the lives of their neighbours. Organizations are set up with the best of aims and ideals and of executive machinery, churches, universities, and charitable institutions which, so long as their income is paid regularly, come to depend for their survival upon the denial of just that element of mutual love and trust, sympathy and friendship, which they were pledged to try and establish. In return for the bread of existence they offer a stone, the kind that holds down the papers at a meeting of some far off Board of Directors, and what wonder, when people come to them in their turn for bread, the bread of knowledge or of spiritual refreshment, they only find a stone.

In such organizations men have become mere numbers.

The love which is truth and the truth which is love are violated. For to accept in theory the law of love, but to deny it in practice as impracticable today, is not to accept it at all. This is happening wherever men use men as tools, as a means to some further end in which these tools have no part, lot of interest, and where they fail to recognize in their fellow beings a common inheritance of a common humanity.

Through love, the love of a Nandini for a Ranjan, it is possible to accept any gift from man, even his death for your sake. But the moment it becomes necessary for us to depend upon men on any other basis, then it is well for us to walk with caution. We are treading upon holy ground without removing our shoes. Without our knowing what is happening the nails in our shoes grind the life under our feet to dust. We walk rough-shod over our neighbours without realizing that humanity and truth have been violated.

It is to this insensibility and to the growth in size of all the ramifications of society that our misery is due. If man were wise he would set to work to discover some common denomination whereby this reduction of life by fractions into death might be prevented for ever. If his intelligence is no longer capable of facing this truth, he must be prepared to face complete entombment and disintegration under the very ramifications which he has himself set up to ward off the day of wrath.

This does not mean that it is necessary for him to cultivate friendship with every individual he meets, but rather that he should extend to all human beings with whom he has any connection, direct or indirect, the same civility and courtesy which he ordinarily reserves for strangers or servants. Civility with friends is not necessary, for, as friendship grows by mutual giving, all barriers break down. Whilst the barrier of strangeness remains, civility or courtesy, is essential. It was this courtesy which made something great of the battles of olden time, but which, now lost, has started the whole human race on a downward path. Once man disdains this courtesy towards his fellows and refuses to use it as a law, seasoning whereby all human relationship becomes palatable, the human soul suffers torture. Misery arises and real friendship, that springs up so easily from a basis of courtesy, becomes impossible.

The sun shines upon us all and rules this material world with its light, the light that is life. Where the sun does not penetrate we light our lamp or turn the switch, but we prefer the rays of the sun, which give us a light, a life, a "sunshine" that the electric bulb can never supply.

So in the world of man it is upon the light of love that we are dependent for human sunshine, for life and joy and beauty, for the "good life". There are regions in our daily life where our touch with our fellows is so meager that this light does not penetrate, and we have to fall back on courtesy. The tip itself, handed surreptitiously to porter or waiter, is a recognition of the fact that, however efficient the machine with which we are momentarily in contact, direct human service demands direct human recognition and so it has become the civil thing to do. We do it surreptitiously because the management has warned us that their organization and remuneration are so efficient, that it has reduced to the lowest fraction the need for human contact, that such a custom is not only unnecessary but even illegal. Such is the complication of life today that most of our money, which is the measure of our power over our fellows, "changes hands" as we say, without those hands ever coming into civil much less friendly contact. We sign cheques, we drop money into slots, and we push it through pigeon holes, where a hand but no face takes charge of it. Through our failure to light the lamp of civility, where the sunshine of friendship cannot reach, we hurt ourselves at the same time as we deprive others of their self-respect, and deny to them their own human significance.

Into a loveless world, a world where men have ceased ever to be civil, a world of "foreign investment," comes Nandini, the embodiment of that light that is beauty and love. She represents the highest truth in the human world, in the nature of man, a truth for which all down the ages, the great have lived, suffered and even died. She too is willing to suffer torture, a death, a mental crucifixion. In losing her lover and her own life she loses her all to save all, the truth of love, for humanity. She offer herself for Ranjan, for love has life in its keep.

So it is that, according to the measure in which we fail to reach this relationship of love in our relations with our fellow men, our life is incomplete. We suffer, we do not deserve peace if we cannot afford to love. And thus men organize themselves for all kinds of ends, excellent in themselves, but fail to recognize this root principle of love that is truth, of truth that is love, in their politics, their worship, their education, their business, their investments, their imperialisms. Just so long will they be incapable of progress, just so long will they tread the path of inevitable destruction. Nature is never so impatient as with those who would divest her of her beauty for selfish ends. Without a common love, a common appreciation of all that is good in man and in the world, it is easy for some tyrant force to find entry, to assert supremacy and to overthrow the little good that remains in a general destruction.

The problem is simple, the cure is simple, so simple that we have grown clever enough not to see it. The highest goal of all is love; a love that each of us is still able to recognize and appreciate, not an obstruction and not an organization, but a spirit, a truth for which men, in all times and countries, have been willing and eager to make the supreme sacrifice, believing that behind this spirit in man, which can be felt, almost touched, lay an objective background which they termed God. To them God was Love. In this God it was possible and easy for all men to find a fundamental union, which was truth. Even if we do not believe in this God, or in any God, yet our experience in home, or family, or community, or country, tells us that love is truth.

The diggers, the King, the Governor, these were men who had no love for the medium in which they worked, for the soil that they were bent upon exploiting. In their efforts they never hesitated to litter the earth with their ugly piles of rubbish in the name of progress. Yet the law of love holds good in the world of nature as well as in the world of man. It is through love for the soil, and for the cherishing of it, that the soil responds to our touch. At that touch our own hurt is healed. In mutilating the soil, that source of beauty that is also wealth, we mutilate ourselves. It was the same soil that these simple villagers had cherished, cultivated and loved, out of which they had grown and produced their needs of livelihood, food, clothes and implements. In it they were now digging their own damnation in service to the god of greed, of profit making, but no longer to the ideal of mutual co-operation and love. Until Nandini came they had not realized that "the times were out of joint" or that there was any more human mode of existence. They accepted their surroundings as King, Priest, Professor and Governor ordered or taught. They took for granted the perpetual domination of the strong, the continued oppression of the weak, and that, in the effort to pile up material wealth, they should, by their own fellows, be transformed from men into machineries, to the mutilation of their own humanity.

Suddenly in the face of this vision of truth, of beauty and of love, the "perfect love which casteth our fear", they realized the greatness of their deprivation. Snatched from her village and her love to satisfy the self-indulgence of the King, to be dissected into her several component parts and analyzed, her hands, her soul, her body and her brain, each with its own. 'marketable value, each capable of being turned to some "useful" purpose in the adding up of wealth, she defeated all by spreading an atmosphere of love wherever she went, in the study of the "dry-as-dust" Professor, lost in his maze of facts, in the office of the file-grinding Governor, even in the room where the policemen kept their thumb-mark register and their card index catalogue. There were of course some who had by long pruning lost all sensibility to love and beauty who had developed a crookedness which could only recognize love as sentiment, and beauty, as effeminacy, who had feasted their souls upon the ugly until they had become suspicious of anything so naked as the truth. Since ugliness is a lie, as lack of civility is a lie, and is a refusal to recognize that beauty is truth as well as love, so beauty itself is invincible. Had the King failed to break the flag-staff with his own hand, it would have been merely a question of time before the very foundations of his vast structure would have been sapped and brought crashing to the ground by the invincible truth of love.

Perfection of order, of law, of government, of empire, of organization in church and state, society or commerce, this is the perfection of machinery and not the creation of happiness. Like the red oleander flower happiness too must be the fruit of love, of labour that is true, that is civil, that is honest, the fruit of human sympathy and consideration, and of human sacrifice in the cause of that real unity which is truth.

Red Oleanders

I

*The curtain rises on a window
covered by a network of intricate pattern in front of the
Palace.* **Nandini** *and* **Kishor,** *a digger boy, come in.*

Kishor.	Have you enough flowers, Nandini? Here, I have brought some more.
Nandini.	Run away, Kishor, do,—back to your work, quick! You'll be late again.
Kishor.	I must steal some time from my digging and digging of nuggets to bring out flowers to you.
Nandini.	But they'll punish you, my boy, if they know.

Kishor.   You said you must have red oleanders.
                 I am glad they're hard to find in this place,
                 Only one tree. I discovered after days
                 of search, nearly hidden away behind a
                 rubbish heap.

Nandini.   Show it to me. I'll go and gather the
                 flowers myself.

Kishor.   Don't be cruel, Nandini. This tree is one
                 of my secret which none shall know. I've
                 always envied Bishu, he can sing to you
                 songs that are his own. From now I shall
                 have flowers which you'll have to take
                 only from my hands.

Nandini.   But it breaks my heart to know that those
                 brutes punish you.

Kishor.   It makes these flowers all the more
                 preciously mine. They come from my pain.

Nandini.   It pains me to accept anything which
                 brings you hurt.

Kishor.	I dream of dying one day for your sake, Nandini.
Nandini.	Is there nothing I can give you in return?
Kishor.	Promise that you will accept flowers only from me every morning.
Nandini.	I will. But do be careful.
Kishor.	No, no, I shall be rash and defy your blows. My homage shall be my daily triumph. [*Goes.*]

Professor *comes in.*

Professor.	Nandini!
Nandini.	Yes, Professor!
Professor.	Why do you come and startle one, now and again, and then pass by? Since you awaken a cry in our hearts, what harm if you stop a moment in answer to it? Let us talk a little.

Nandini.   What need have you of me?

Professor.   If you talk of need, look over there!—You'll see our tunnel-diggers creeping out of the holes like worms, with loads of things in need. In this Yaksha town all our treasure is of gold, the secret treasure of dust. But the gold which is you, beautiful one, is not of the dust, but of the light which never owns any bond.

Nandini.   Over and over again you say this to me, What makes you wonder at me so, Professor?

Professor.   The sunlight gleaming through the forest thickets surprises nobody, but the light that breaks through a cracked wall is quite a different thing. In Yaksha town, you are this light that startles. Tell me, what d'you think of this place?

Nandini.   It puzzles me to see a whole city thrusting its head underground, groping with both hands in the dark. You dig tunnels in the underworld and come out with dead wealth that the earth has kept buried for ages past.

Professor. The *Jinn* of that dead wealth we invoke. If we can enslave him the whole world lies at our feet.

Nandini. Then again, you hide your king behind a wall of netting. Is it for fear of people finding out that he's a man?

Professor. As the ghost of our dead wealth is fearfully potent so is our ghostly royalty, made hazy by this net, with its inhuman power to frighten people.

Nandini. All you say is a kind of made-up talk.

Professor. Of course made-up. The naked is without a credential, it's the made-up clothes that define us. It delights me immensely to discuss philosophy with you.

Nandini.	That's strange! You who burrow day and night in a mass of yellow pages, like your diggers in the bowels of the earth,—why waste your time on me?
Professor.	The privilege of wasting time proves one's wealth of time. We poor drudges are insects in a hole in this solid toil, you are the evening star in the rich sky of leisure. When we see you, our wings grow restless. Come to my room. For a moment allow me to be reckless in my waste of time.
Nandini.	No, not now. I have come to see your king, in his room.
Professor.	How can you enter through the screen?
Nandini.	I shall find my way through the net-work.
Professor.	Do you know, Nandini, I too live behind a net-work of scholarship. I am an unmitigated scholar, just as our king is an unmitigated king.

Nandini.   You are laughing at me, Professor. But tell me, when they brought me here, why did'nt they bring my Ranjan also?

Professor.   It's their way to snatch things by fractions. But why should you want to drag your life's treasure down amongst this dead wealth of ours?

Nandini.   Because I know he can put a beating heart behind these dead ribs.

Professor.   Your own presence is puzzling enough for our governors here; if Ranjan also comes they will be in despair.

Nandini.   They do not know how comic they are,— Ranjan will bring God's own laughter in their midst and startle them into life.

Professor.   Divine laughter is the sunlight that melts ice, but not stones. Only the pressure of gross muscle can' move our governors.

Nandini.   My Ranjan's strength is like that of your river, Sankhini,—it can laugh and yet it can break. Let me tell you a little secret news of mine. I shall meet Ranjan to-day.

Professor.   Who told you that?

Nandini.   Yes, yes, we shall meet. The news has come.

Professor.	Through what way could news come and yet evade the Governor?
Nandini.	Through the same way that brings news of the coming Spring.
Professor.	You mean it's in the air,—like the rumours which flush in the colour of the sky, or flutter in the dance of the wind?
Nandini.	I won't say more now. When Ranjan comes you'll see for yourself how rumours in the air come down on earth.
Professor.	Once she begins to talk of Ranjan there's no stopping Nandini's mouth! Well, well, I have my books, let me take my shelter behind them,—I dare not go on with this. [*Coming back after going a little way.*] Nandini. Let me ask you one thing. Aren't you frightened of our Yaksha Town?
Nandini.	Why should I feel afraid?

Professor.   All creatures fear an eclipse, not the full
                sun. Yaksha Town is a city under eclipse.
                The Shadow Demon, who lives in the gold
                caves, has eaten into it. It is not whole
                itself, neither does it allow anyone else to
                remain whole. Listen to me, don't stay here.
                When you go, these pits will yawn all the
                wider for us, I know,—yet I say to you, fly;
                go and live happily with Ranjan where
                people in their drunken fury don't tear
                the earth's veil to pieces. [*Going a little
                way and then coming back.*] Nandini, will
                you give me a flower from your chain of
                red oleanders?

Nandini.   Why, what will you do with it?

Professor.   How often have I thought that there is
                some omen in these ornaments of yours.

Nandini.   I don't know of any.

Professor.   Perhaps your fate knows. In that red there is
                not only beauty, but also the fascination of fear.

Nandini.   Fear! Even in me?

Professor.   I don't know what event you have come to write with that crimson tint. There was the gardenia and the tuberose, there was white jasmine, —why did you leave them all and choose this flower? Do you know, we often choose our own fate thus, without knowing it!

Nandini.   Ranjan sometimes calls me Red Oleander. I feel that the colour of his love is red,— that red I wear on my neck, on my breast, on my arms.

Professor.   Well, just give me one of those flowers,—a moment's gift,—let me try to understand the meaning of its colour.

Nandini.   Here, take it. Ranjan is coming to-day,— out of my heart's delight I give it to you.

                              [*Professor goes.*]

Gokul, *a digger, comes in.*

Gokul.   Turn this way, woman! Who are you? I've never yet been able to understand you.

Nandini.   I'm nothing more than what you see. What need have you to understand me?

Gokul.   I don't trust what I can't understand. For what purpose has the King brought you here?

Nandini.   Because I serve no purpose of his.

Gokul.   You know some spell, I'm sure. You're snaring everybody here. You're a witch! Those who are bewitched by your beauty will come to their death.

Nandini.   That death will not be yours, Gokul, never fear! You'll die digging.

Gokul.   Let-me see, let me see, what's that dangling over your forehead?

Nandini.   Only a tassel of red oleanders.

Gokul. What does it mean?

Nandini. It has no meaning at all.

Gokul. I don't believe you, one bit! You're up to some trickery. Some evil will befall us before the day is out. That's why you have got yourself up like this. Oh you terrible, terrible witch!

Nandini. What makes you think me so terrible?

Gokul. You're looking like an ominous torch.

Nandini. The autumn song:
Hark, 'tis Autumn calling:
'Come, O, come away!'—
Her basket is heaped with corn.
Don't you see the September sun is spreading the glow of the ripening corn in the air?
Drunken with the perfumed
wine of wind, shivering corn,
its sunlight trailing, on the field

You too come out, King!—out into the fields.

Voice.   Fields! What could I do there?

Nandini.   The work there is much simpler than your work in Yaksha Town.

Voice.   It's the simple which is impossible for me. A lake cannot run out dancing, like a frolicsome waterfall. Leave me now, I have no time.

Nandini.   The day you let me into your store-house the blocks of gold did not surprise me, —what amazed me was the immense strength with which you lifted and arranged them. But can blocks of gold ever answer to the swinging rhythm of your arms in the same way as fields of corn? Are you not afraid, King, of handling the dead wealth of the earth?

Voice.   What is there to fear?

Nandini.	The living heart of the earth gives itself up in love and life and beauty, but when you rend its bosom and disturb the dead, you bring up with your booty the curse of its dark demon, blind and hard, cruel and envious. Don't you see everybody here is either angry, or suspicious, or afraid?
Voice.	Curse?
Nandini.	Yes, the curse of grabbing and killing.
Voice.	But we bring up strength. Does not my strength please you, Nandini?
Nandini.	Indeed it does. Therefore I ask you, come out into the light, step on the ground, let the earth be glad.
Voice.	Do you know, Nandini, you too are half-hidden behind an evasion,—you mystery of beauty! I want to pluck you out of it, to grasp you within my closed fist, to handle you, scrutinise you,—or else to break you to pieces.

Nandini.   Whatever do you mean?

Voice.   Why can't I strain out the tint of your
                  oleanders and build a dream out of it to
                  keep before my eyes? Those few frail petals
                  guard it and hinder me. Within you there
                  is the same hindrance, so strong because
                  so soft. Nandini, will you tell me what you
                  think of me?

Nandini.   Not now, you have no time. Let me go.

Voice.   No, no, don't go. Do tell me what you
                  think of me.

Nandini.   Have I not told you often enough? I think
                  you are wonderful. Strength swelling
                  up in your arms, like rolling clouds
                  before a storm,—it makes my heart dance
                  within me.

Voice.   And when your heart dances to see Ranjan,
                  is that also—

Nandini.	Let that be,—you have no time.
Voice.	There is time,—for this; only tell me, then go.
Nandini.	That dance rhythm is different, you won't understand.
Voice.	I will, I must understand.
Nandini.	I can't explain it clearly. Let me go.
Voice.	Tell me, at least, whether you like me.
Nandini.	Yes, I like you.
Voice.	The same as Ranjan?
Nandini.	Again the same question! I tell you, you don't understand these things.
Voice.	I *do* understand, a little. I know what the difference is between Ranjan and me. In me there is only strength, in Ranjan there is magic.

Nandini.   What d'you mean by magic?

Voice.   Shall I explain? Underground there are blocks of stone, iron, gold,—there you have the image of strength. On the surface grows the grass, the flower blossoms,—there you have the play of magic. I can extract gold from the fearsome depths of secrecy, but to wrest that magic from the near at hand I fail.

Nandini.   You have no end of things, yet why always covet?

Voice.   All I possess is so much dead weight. No increase of gold can create a particle of a touchstone, no increase of power can ever come up to youth. I can only guard by force. If I had Ranjan's youth I could leave you free and yet hold you fast. My time is spent in knotting the binding rope, but, alas, everything else can be kept tied, except joy.

Nandini.   It is you who entangle yourself in your own net, then why keep on fretting?

Voice.   You will never understand. I, who am a desert, stretch out my hand to you, a tiny blade of grass, and cry: I am parched, I am bare, I am weary. The flaming thirst of this desert licks up one fertile field after another, only to enlarge itself—it can never annex the life of the frailest of grasses.

Nandini.   One would never think you were so tired.

Voice.   One day, Nandini in a far off land, I saw a mountain as weary as myself. I could not guess that all its stones were aching inwardly. One night I heard a noise, as if some giant's evil dream had moaned and moaned and suddenly snapped asunder. Next morning I found the mountain had disappeared in the chasm of a yawning earthquake. That made me understand how overgrown power crushes itself inwardly

	by its own weight. I see in you something quite opposite.
Nandini.	What is it you see in me?
Voice.	The dance rhythm of the All.
Nandini.	I don't understand.
Voice.	The rhythm that lightens the enormous weight of matter. To that rhythm the bands of stars and planets go about dancing from sky to sky, like so many minstrel boys. It is that rhythm,
Nandini.	That makes you so simple, so perfect. How small you are compared to me, yet I envy you.
Nandini.	You have cut yourself off from everybody and so deprived yourself.
Voice.	I keep myself apart, that it may become easy for me to plunder the world's big

treasure-houses. Nevertheless there are gifts that your little flower-like fingers can easily reach, but not all the strength of my body,—gifts hidden in God's closed hand. That hand I must force open some day.

Nandini. When you talk like that, I don't follow you. Let me go.

Voice. Go then; but here, I stretch out this hand of mine from my window, place your hand on it for a moment.

Nandini. Only a hand, and the rest of you hidden? It frightens me!

Voice. Everybody flies from me because they only see my hand. But if I wished to hold you with all of me, would you come to me, Nandini?

Nandini. Why talk like this when you wouldn't even let me come in to your room?

Voice.   My busy time, overloaded with work, dragged along against obstruction, is not for you. On the day when you can arrive, full sail before the wind, into the bosom of my full.

Phagulal.   Isn't it our holiday? Yesterday was the fast day of the War Goddess. To-day they worship the Flag.

Chandra.   Must you drink just because it's a holiday? In our village home, on feast days, you never—

Phagulal.   Freedom itself was enough for the holidays in our village. The caged bird spends its holiday knocking against the bars. In Yaksha Town holidays are more of a nuisance than work.

Chandra.   Let's go back home, then.

Phagulal.   The road to our home is closed for ever.

Chandra.   How's that?

Phagulal.   Our homes don't yield them any profit.

Chandra.   But are we closely fitted to their profits only,—like husks to grains of corn, —with nothing of us left over?

Phagulal.   Our mad Bishu says: to remain whole is useful only for the lamb itself; those who eat it prefer to leave out its horns and hooves, and even object to its bleating when butchered. There's the madcap, singing as he goes.

Chandra.   It's only the last few days that his songs have burst forth.

Phagulal.   That's true.

Chandra.   He's been possessed by Nandini. She draws his heart and his songs too.

Phagulal.   No wonder.

Chandra.   Indeed! You'd better be careful, She'll next
                 be bringing out songs from *your* throat,—
                 which would be rough on our neighbours.
                 The witch is up to all kinds of tricks, and
                 is sure to bring misfortune.

Phagulal.   Bishu's misfortune is nothing recent, he
                 knew Nandini long before coming here.

Chandra   I say, Bishu, come this way. Maybe you'll
[calling out]. find somebody here also to listen to
                 your singing,—it won't be altogether
                 thrown away.

Bishu *comes in, singing.*

Bishu [sings].   *Boatman of my dreams,*
                 The sail is filled with a boisterous breeze
                          and my mad heart sings
                     to the lilt of the rocking of thy boat,
                   at the call of the far away landing.

Chandra.   I know who the boatman of your
                 dreams is.

Bishu.	How should you know from outside? You haven't seen from inside my boat.
Chandra.	Your boat is going to get wrecked one of these days, let me tell you, —by that pet Nandini of yours.

Gokul, *the digger, comes in.*

Gokul.	I say, Bishu, I don't quite trust your Nandini.
Bishu.	Why, what has she done?
Gokul.	She does nothing, that's the rub. I don't understand the way she goes on.
Chandra.	To see her flaunting her prettiness all over the place makes me sick.
Gokul.	We can trust features that are plain enough to understand.
Bishu.	I know the atmosphere of this place

breeds contempt for beauty. There must be beauty even in hell; but nobody there can understand it, that's their cruellest punishment.

Chandra.   Maybe we are fools, but even our Governor here can't stand her—d'you know that?

Bishu.   Take care, Chandra, lest you catch the infection of our Governor's eyes—then perhaps yours too will redden at the sight of us. What say you, Phagulal?

Phagulal.   To tell you the truth, brother, when I see Nandini, I feel ashamed to think of myself. I can't utter a word when she's there.

Gokul.   The day will come when you'll know her to your cost,—perhaps too late.

                                        [*Goes.*]

Phagulal.   Bishu, your friend Chandra wants to know why we drink.

Bishu.   God in his mercy has everywhere provided a liberal allowance of drink. We men with our arms supply the output of our muscles, you women with yours supply the wine of embraces. In this world there is hunger to force us to work; but there's also the green of the woods, the gold of the sunshine, to make us drunk with their holiday-call.

Chandra.   You call these things *drink*?

Bishu.   Yes, drinks of life, an endless stream of intoxication. Take my case. I come to this place; I am set to work burgling the underworld; for me nature's own ration of spirits is stopped; so my inner man craves the artificial wine of the market place.

[Sings.]

My life, your sap has run dry,
Fill then the cup with the wine of
death,
That flushes all emptiness with its
laughter.

Chandra.   Come, brother, let us fly from here.

Bishu.   To that boundless tavern, underneath the
                  blue canopy? Alas, the road is closed, and
                  we seek consolation in the stolen wine of
                  the prison house. No open sky: no leisure
                  for us; so we have distilled he essence of
                  all the song and laughter, all the sunlight
                  of the twelve hours' day into one draught
                  of liquid fire.

                  [Sings.]

                  Thy sun is hidden amid a mass
                  of murky cloud.
                  Thy day has smudged itself
                  black in dusty toil.
                  Then let the dark night descend
                  the last comrade of drunken
                  oblivion,
                  Let it cover thy tired eyes with
                  the mist
                  that will help thee desperately to
                  lose thyself.

Chandra.   Well, well, Bishu, you men have gone to

the dogs in Yaksha Town, if you like, but we women haven't changed at all.

Bishu. Haven't you? Your flowers have faded, and you are all slavering for gold.

Chandra. No, never!

Bishu. I say, yes. That Phagulal toils for hours over and above the twelve,—why? For a reason unknown to him, unknown even to you. But I know. It's your dream of gold that lashes him on to work, more severely than the foreman's whip.

Chandra. Very well. Then why don't we fly from here, and go back home?

Bishu. Your Governor has closed the way as well as the will to return. If you go there to-day you will fly back here to-morrow, like a caged bird to its cage, hankering for its drugged food.

Phagulal.   I say, Bishu, once upon a time you came very near spoiling your eyesight poring over books; how is it they made you ply the spade along with the rest of us stupid boors?

Chandra.   All this time we've been here, we haven't got from Bishu the answer to this particular question.

Phagulal.   Yet we all know it.

Bishu.   Well, out with it then!

Phagulal.   They employed you to spy on us.

Bishu.   If you knew that, how is it you let me off alive?

Phagulal.   But, we knew also, that game was not in your line.

Chandra.   How is it you couldn't stick to such a comfortable job, brother?

Bishu.   Comfortable job? To stick to a living being
                     like a carbuncle on his back?

                     I said: 'I must go home, my health is
                     failing.' 'Poor thing,' said the Governor,
                     'how can you go home in such a state?
                     However. there's no harm in your trying.'

                     Well, I dip try. And then I found that, as
                     soon as one enters the maw of Yaksha
                     Town, its jaws shut fast, and the one road
                     that remains open leads withinwards. Now
                     I am swamped in that interior without hope
                     and without light, and the only difference
                     between you and me is, that the Governor
                     looks down upon me even worse than upon
                     you. Man despises the broken pot of his
                     own creation more than the withered leaf
                     fallen from the tree.

Phagulal.   What does that matter, Bishu? You have
                     risen high in our esteem.

Bishu.   Discovery only means death. Where you
                     favour falls there falls the Governor's glance.
                     The more noisily the yellow frogs welcome

the black toad, the sooner their croaking points him out to the boa-constrictor.

Chandra. But when will your work be finished?

Bishu. The calendar never records the last day. After the first day comes the second, after the second the third. There's no such thing as getting finished here. We're always digging—one yard, two yards, three yards. We go on raising gold nuggets,—after one nugget another, then more and more and more. In Yaksha Town figures follow one another in rows and never arrive at any conclusion. That's why we are not men to them, but only numbers.—Phagu, what's yours?

Phagulal. I'm No. 47 V.

Bishu. I'm 69 Ng.

Chandra. Brother, they've hoarded such heaps of gold, can't they stop digging now?

Bishu.	There's always an end to things of need, no doubt; so we stop when we've had enough to eat. But we don't need drunkenness, therefore there's no end to it. These nuggets are the drink—the solid drink—of our Gold King. Don't you see?
Chandra.	No, I don't.
Bishu.	Cups in hand, we forget that we are chained to our limits. Gold blocks in hand, our master fancies he's freed from the gravitation of the commonplace, and is soaring in the rarest of upper heights.
Chandra.	In this season the villages are preparing for their harvest festival. Let's go home.
Phagulal.	Don't worry me; Chandra. A thousand times over have I told you that in these parts there are high roads to the market, to the burning ground, to the scaffold,— everywhere except to the homeland.

Chandra.   If we were to go to the Governor, and just
                tell him—

Bishu.   Hasn't your woman's wit seen through the
                Governor yet?

Chandra.   Why, he seems to be so nice and—

Bishu.   Yes, nice and polished, like the crocodile's
                teeth, which fit into one another with so
                thorough a bite that the King himself can't
                unlock the jaw, even if he wants to.

Chandra.   There comes the Governor.

Bishu.   Then it's all up with us. He's sure to
                have overheard.

Chandra.   Why, we haven't said anything so very—

Bishu.   Sister, we can only say the words, —they
                put in the meaning.

                     The **Governor** *comes in.*

Chandra.   Sir Governor!

Governor.   Well, my child?

Chandra.   Grant us leave to go home for a little. .

Governor.   Why, aren't the rooms we have given you excellent, much better than the ones at home? We have even kept a state watchman for your safety. Hullo, 69 Ng, to see you amongst these people reminds one of a heron come to teach paddy birds how to cut capers.

Bishu.   Sir, your jesting does not reassure me. Had my feet the strength to make others dance, would I not have run away from here, first thing? Especially after the striking examples I've seen of the fate that overtakes dancing masters in this country. As things are, one's legs tremble even to walk straight.

Chandra.   Give us leave, Sir Governor, do give us

leave. Let us go just for once, and see our waving fields of barleycorn in the ear, and the ample shade of our banian tree with its hanging roots. I cannot tell you how our hearts ache. Don't you see that your men here work all day in the dark, and in the evening steep themselves in the denser dark of drunkenness? Have you no pity for them?

Governor.   My dear child, surely you know of our constant anxiety for their welfare. That is exactly why I have sent for our High Preacher, Kenaram Gosain himself, to give moral talks to the men. Their votive fees will pay for his upkeep. Every evening the Gosain will come and—

Phagulal.   That won't do, sir! Now, at worst, we get drunk of an evening, but if we are preached to every night, there'll be manslaughter!

Bishu.   Hush, hush, Phagulal,

Preacher* Gosain *comes in.

Governor.   Talk of the Preacher and he appears.
Your Holiness, I do you reverence. These
workmen of ours sometimes feel disturbed
in their weak minds. Deign to whisper
in their ears some texts of peace. The need
is urgent.

Gosain.   These people? Are they not the very
incarnation of the sacred Tortoise of our
scripture, that held up the sinking earth on
its back? Because they meekly suppress
themselves underneath their burden, the
upper world can keep its head aloft. The
very thought sends a thrill through my
body! Just think of it, friend 47 V, yours
is the duty of supplying food to this mouth
which chants the holy name. With the
sweat of your brow have you woven this
wrap printed with the holy name, which
exalts this devoted body. Surely that is no
mean privilege. May you remain forever
undisturbed, is my benediction, for then

the grace of God will abide with you likewise. My friends repeat aloud the holy name of Hari, and all your burdens will be lightened. The name of Hari shall be taken in the beginning, in the middle, and at the end,—so say the scriptures.

Chandra.   How sweet! It's long since I have heard such words! Give, oh give me a little dust off your feet!

Phagulal.   Stop this waste of money, Governor. If it's our offerings you want, we can stand it, but we're fairly sick of this cant.

Bishu.   Once Phagulal runs amok it's all over with the lot of you. Hush, hush, Phagulal!

Chandra.   Are you bent on spoiling your chances both in this world and the next, you wretched man? You were never like this before. Nandini's ill wind has blown upon you,—and no mistake.

Gosain.	What charming naiveté, Sir Governor! What's in their heart is always on their lips. What can we teach them?—it's they who'll teach us a lesson. You know what I mean.
Governor.	I know where the root of the trouble is. I'll have to take them in hand myself, I see. Meanwhile, pray go to the next parish and chant them the holy name,—the sawyers there have taken to grumbling, somewhat.
Gosain.	Which parish did you say?
Governor.	Parish T-D. No. 71 T is headman there. It ends to the left of where No. 65 of Row M lives.
Gosain.	My son, though Parish T-D may not yet be quieted, the whole Row of M's have lately become steeped in a beautiful spirit of meekness. Still it is better to keep an extra police force posted in the parish some time longer. Because, as you know our

scripture says,—pride is our greatest foe.
After the strength of the police has helped
to conquer pride, then comes our turn. I
take my leave.

Chandra.   Forgive these men, Your Holiness, and
give them your blessing, that they may
follow the right path.

Gosain.   Fear not, good woman, they'll all end
thoroughly pacified.

                              [*The* Gosain *goes.*]

Governor.   I say, 69 Ng, the temper of your parish
seems to be somewhat strained.

Bishu.   That's nothing strange. The Gosain called
them the incarnation of the Tortoise.
But, according to scripture, incarnations
change; and, when the Tortoise gave place
to the Boar, place of hard shell came
out aggressive teeth, so that all—
suffering patience was transformed into
defiant obstinacy.

Chandra.   But, Sir Governor, don't forget my request.

Governor.   I have heard it and will bear it in mind.

[*He goes.*]

Chandra.   Ah now, didn't you see how nice the Governor is? How he smiles every time he talks!

Bishu.   Crocodile's teeth begin by smiling and end by biting.

Chandra.   Where does his bite come in?

Bishu.   Don't you know he's going to make it a rule not to workmen's wives accompany them here.

Chandra.   Why?

Bishu.   We have a place in their account book as numbers, but women's figures do not mate with figures of arithmetic.

Chandra.   O dear! but have they no women-folk of their own?

Bishu.   Their ladies are besotted with the wine of gold, .even worse than their husbands.

Chandra.   Bishu, you had a wife at home,—what's become of her?

Bishu.   So long as I filled the honoured post of spy, they used to invite her to those big mansions to play cards with their ladies. Ever since I joined Phagulal's set, all that was stopped, and she left me in a huff at the humiliation.

Chandra.   For shame! But look, brother Bishu, what a grand procession! One palanquin after another! Don't you see the sparkle of the jewelled fringes of the elephant-seats? How beautiful the out-riders on horseback look, as if they had bits of sunlight pinned on the points of their spears!

Bishu.	Those are the Governor's and Deputy Governor's ladies, going to the Flag-worship.
Chandra.	Bless my soul, what a gorgeous array and how fine they look! I say, Bishu, if you hadn't given up that job, would you have gone along with that set in this grand style?—and that wife of yours surely—
Bishu.	Yes, we too should have come to just such a pass.
Chandra.	Is there no way going back,—none whatever?
Bishu.	There is,—through the gutter.
A Distant Voice.	Bishu, my mad one!
Bishu.	Yes, my mad girl!
Phagulal.	There's Nandini. There'll be no more of Bishu for us, for the rest of the day.

Chandra.	Tell me, Bishu, what does she charm you with?
Bishu.	The charm of sorrow.
Chandra.	Why do you talk so topsy-turvy?
Bishu.	She reminds me that there are sorrows, to forget which is the greatest of sorrow.
Phagulal.	Please to speak plainly, Bishu, otherwise it becomes positively annoying!
Bishu.	The pain of desire for the near belongs to the animal, the sorrow of aspiration for the far belongs to man. That far away flame of my eternal sorrow is revealed through Nandini.
Chandra.	Brother, we don't understand these things. But one thing I do understand and that is, —the less you men can make out a girl, the more she attracts you! We simple women, —our price is not

so high, but we at least keep you on the straight path. I warn you, once for all, that girl with her noose of red oleanders will drag you to perdition.

[Chandra *and* Phagulal *go*.]

Nandini *comes in.*

Nandini.   My mad one, did you hear their autumn songs this morning?

Bishu.   Is my morning like yours that I should hear singing? Mine is only a swept-away remnant of the weary night.

Nandini.   In my gladness of heart I thought I'd stand on the rampart and join in their song. But the guards would not let me, so I've come to you.

Bishu.   I am not a rampart.

Nandini.   You are my rampart. When I come to you I seem to climb high, I find the open light.

Bishu. Ever since coming to Yaksha Town the sky has dropped out of my life. I felt as if they had pounded me in the same mortar with all the fractions of men here, and rolled us into a solid lump. Then you came and looked into my face in a way that made me sure some light could still be seen through me.

Nandini. In this closed fort a bit of sky survives only between you and me, my mad one.

Bishu. Through that sky my songs can fly towards you.

[Sings.]

You keep me awake that I may
sing to you,
O Breaker of my sleep!
And so my heart you startle with
your call,
O Waker of my grief!
The shades of evening fall,
the birds come to their nest.
The boat arrives ashore,

> *yet my heart knows no rest,*
> *O Waker of my grief!*

Nandini.   The waker of your grief, Bishu?

Bishu.   Yes, you are my messenger from the unreachable shore. The day you came to Yaksha Town a gust of salt air knocked at my heart.

Nandini.   But I never had any message of this sorrow of which you sing.

Bishu.   Not even from Ranjan?

Nandini.   No, he holds an oar in each hand and ferries me across the stormy waters; he catches wild horses by the mane and rides with me through the woods; he shoots an arrow between the eyebrows of the tiger on the spring, and scatters my fear with loud laughter. As he jumps into our Nagai river and disturbs its current with his

joyous splashing, so he disturbs me with
his tumultuous life. Desperately he stakes
his all on the game and thus has he won
me. You also were there with us, but you
held aloof, and at last something urged you
one day to leave our gambling set. At the
time of your parting you looked at my face
in a way I could not quite make out. After
that I've had no news of you for long. Tell
me where you went off to then.

Bishu.   My boat was tied to the bank; the rope
                snapped; the wild wind drove it into the
                tackles unknown.

Nandini.   But who dragged you back from there to
                dig for nuggets here in Yaksha Town?

Bishu.   A woman. Just as a bird on the wing is
                brought to the ground by a chance arrow,
                so did she bring me down to the dust. I
                forgot myself.

Nandini.   How could she touch you?

Bishu.	When the thirsty heart despairs of finding water it's easy enough for it to be deluded by a mirage, and driven in barren quest from desert to desert. One day, while I was gazing at the sunset clouds, she had her eye upon the golden spire of the Governor's palace. Her glance challenged me to take her over there. In my foolish pride I vowed to do so. When I did bring her here, under the golden spire, the spell was broken.
Nandini.	I've come to take you away from here.
Bishu.	Since you have moved even the king of this place, what power on earth can prevent you? Tell me, don't you feel afraid of him?
Nandini.	I did fear him from outside that screen. But now I've seen him inside.
Bishu.	What was he like?
Nandini.	Like a man from the epics,—his forehead

like the gateway of a tower, his arms the iron bolts of some inaccessible fortress.

Bishu.   What did you see when you went inside?

Nandini.   A falcon was sitting on his left wrist. He put it on the perch and gazed at my face. Then just as he had been stroking the falcon's wings, he began gently to stroke my hand. After a while he suddenly asked: 'Don't you fear me, Nandini?'
'Not in the least,' said I.
Then he buried his fingers in my unbound hair and sat long with closed eyes.

Bishu.   How did you like it?

Nandini.   I liked it. Shall I tell you how? It was as if he were a thousand-year-old banyan tree, and I a tiny little bird; when I lit on a branch of his and had my little swing, he needs must have felt a thrill of delight to his very marrow. I loved to give that bit of joy to that lonely soul.

Bishu.   Then what did he say?

Nandini.   Starting up and fixing his spear-point gaze on my face, he suddenly said: 'I want to know you.'

I felt a shiver run down my body and asked: 'What is there to know?—I am not a manuscript!'

'I know all there is in manuscripts,' said he, 'but I don't know you.' Then he became excited and cried: 'Tell me all about Ranjan. Tell me how you love him.'

I talked on: 'I love Ranjan as the rudder in the water might love the sail in the sky, answering its rhythm of wind in the rhythm of waves.'

He listened quietly, staring like a big greedy boy. All of a sudden he startled me by exclaiming: 'Could you die for him?'

'This very moment,' I replied.

'Never,' he almost roared, as if in anger.

'Yes, I could,' I repeated.

'What good would that do you?'

'I don't know,' said I.

Then he writhed and shouted: 'Go away from my room, go, go at once, don't disturb me in my work.'

I could not understand what that meant.

Bishu.   He gets angry when he can't understand.

Nandini.   Bishu, don't you feel pity for him?

Bishu.   The day when God will be moved to pity for him, he will die.

Nandini.   No, no, you don't know how desperately he wants to live.

Bishu.   You will see this very day what his living means. I don't know whether you'll be able to bear the sight.

Nandini.   There, look, there's a shadow. I am sure the Governor has secretly heard what we've been saying.

Bishu.	This place is dark with the Governor's shadow, it is every- where. How do you like him?
Nandini.	I have never seen anything so lifeless—like a cane stick cut from the cane bush,—no leaves, no roots, no sap in the veins.
Bishu.	Cut off from life, he spends himself in repressing life.
Nandini.	Hush, he will hear you.
Bishu.	He hears even when you are silent, which is all the more dangerous. When I am with the diggers I am careful in my speech, so much so that the Governor thinks I'm the sorriest of the lot, and spares me out of sheer contempt. But, my mad girl, when I am with you my mind scorns to be cautious.
Nandini.	No, no, you must not court danger. There comes the Governor.

Rabindranath Tagore

The* Governor *comes in.

Governor.   Hallo, 69 Ng! you seem to be making friends with everybody, without distinction.

Bishu.   You may remember that I began by making friends even with you, only it was the distinction that stood in the way.

Governor.   Well, what are we discussing now?

Bishu.   We are discussing how to escape from this fortress of yours.

Governor.   Really? So recklessly, that you don't even mind confessing it?

Bishu.   Sir Governor, it doesn't need much cleverness to know that when a captive bird pecks at the bars it's not in the spirit of caress. What does it matter whether that's openly confessed or not?

Governor.   The captives' want of love we were aware

of, but their not fearing to admit it has become evident only recently.

Nandini. Won't you let Ranjan come?

Governor. You will see him this very day.

Nandini. I knew that; still, for your message of hope I wish you victory. Governor, take this garland of *kunda* flowers.

Governor. Why throw away the garland thus, and not keep it for Ranjan?

Nandini. There is a garland for him.

Governor. Aha, I thought so! I suppose it's the one hanging round your neck. The garland of victory may be of *kunda* flowers, the gift of the hand; but the garland of welcome is of red oleanders, the gift of the heart. Well, let's be quick in accepting what comes from the hand, for that will fade; as for the heart's offering, the longer it waits the more precious it grows.

[*The* Governor *goes*.]

Nandini [*knocking at the window*].	Do you hear? Let me come into your room.
Voice [*from behind the scenes*].	Why always the same futile request? Who is that with you? A pair to Ranjan?
Bishu.	No, King, I am the obverse side of Ranjan, on which falls the shadow.
Voice.	What use has Nandini for you?
Bishu.	The use which music has for the hollow of the flute.
Voice.	Nandini, what is this man to you?
Nandini.	He's my partner in music. My heart soars in his voice, my pain cries in his tunes,— that's what he tells me.

[*Sings.*]

'I love, I love,'—Tis the cry that
breaks out
from the bosom of earth and
water.

Voice.	So that's your partner! What if I dissolved your partnership this very minute?
Nandini.	Why are you so cross? Haven't you any companion yourself?
Voice.	Has the mid-day sun any companion?
Nandini.	Well, let's change the subject. What's that? What's that in your hand?
Voice.	A dead frog.
Nandini.	What for?
Voice.	Once upon a time this frog got into a hole in a stone, and in that shelter it existed for three thousand years. I have learnt from it

the secret of continuing to exist, but to live it does not know. To-day I felt bored and smashed its shelter. I've thus saved it from existing forever. Isn't that good news?

Nandini.   Your stone walls will also fall away from around me to-day,—I shall meet Ranjan.

Voice.   I want to see you both together.

Nandini.   You won't be able to see from behind your net.

Voice.   I shall let you sit inside my room.

Nandini.   What will you do with us?

Voice.   Nothing, I only want to know you.

Nandini.   When you talk of knowing, it frightens me.

Voice.   Why?

Nandini.   I feel that you have no patience with things that cannot be known, but can only be felt.

Voice.   I dare not trust such things lest they should play me false. Now go away, don't waste my time.—No, no, wait a little. Give me that tassel of red oleanders which hangs from your hair.

Nandini.   What will you do with it?

Voice.   When I look at those flowers it seems to me as if the red light of my evil star has appeared in their shape. At times I want to snatch them from you and tear them to pieces. Again I think that if Nandini were ever to place that spray of flowers on my head, with her own hands, then—

Nandini.   Then what?

Voice.   Then perhaps I might die in peace.

Nandini.   Someone loves red oleanders and calls me by that name. It is in remembrance of him that I wear these flowers.

Voice.   Then, I tell you, they're going to be *his* evil
                star as well as *mine*.

Nandini.   Don't say such things for shame!
                I am going.

Voice.   Where?

Nandini.   I shall go and sit near the gate of
                your fort.

Voice.   Why?

Nandini.   When Ranjan comes he'll see I am waiting
                for him.

Voice.   I should like to tread hard on Ranjan and
                grind him in the dust.

Nandini.   Why pretend to frighten me?

Voice.   Pretend, you say? Don't you know I am
                really fearsome?

Nandini.   You seem to take pleasure in seeing people

frightened at you. In our village plays Srikantha takes the part of a demon; when he comes on the stage, he is delighted if the children are terrified. You are like him. Do you know what I think?

Voice.   What is it?

Nandini.   The people here trade on frightening others. That's why they have put you behind a network and dressed you fantastically. Don't you feel ashamed to be got up like a bogeyman?

Voice.   How dare you!

Nandini.   Those whom you have scared all along will one day feel ashamed to be afraid. If my Ranjan were here, he would have snapped his fingers in your face, and not been afraid even if he died for it.

Voice.   Your impudence is something great. I should like to stand you up on the top of a heap of everything I've smashed throughout my life. And then—

Nandini.   Then what?

Voice.   Then, like a squeezed bunch of grapes with its juice running out from between the gripping fingers, if I could but hold you tight with these two hands of mine,—and then—go, go, run away, at once, at once!

Nandini.   If you shout at me so rudely, I'll stay on, do what you will!

Voice.   I long savagely to prove to you how cruel I am. Have you never heard moans from inside my room?

Nandini.   I have. Whose moaning was it?

Voice.   The hidden mystery of life, wrenched away by me, bewails its torn ties. To get fire from a tree you have to burn it. Nandini, there is fire within you too, red fire. One day I shall burn you and extract that also.

Nandini. Oh, you are cruel!

Voice. I must either gather or scatter. I can feel no pity for what I do not get. Breaking is a fierce kind of getting.

Nandini. But why thrust out your clenched fist like that?

Voice. Here, I take away my fist. Now fly, as the dove flies from the shadow of a hawk.

Nandini. Very well, I will go, and not vex you anymore.

Voice. Here, listen, come back, Nandini!

Nandini. What is it?

Voice. On your face, there is the play of life in your eyes and lips; at the back of you flows your black hair, the silent fall of death. The other day when my hands sank into it they felt the *soft calm of dying*. I long to sleep with my face hidden inside those thick black clusters. You don't know how tired I am!

Nandini.   Don't you ever sleep?

Voice.   I feel afraid to sleep.

Nandini.   Let me sing you the latest song that I've learnt.
               [*Sings.*]
                   'I love, I love' is the cry that
                       breaks out from
                   the bosom of earth and water.
                       The sky broods like an aching
                       heart, the horizon is
                   tender like eyes misted with
                       tears.

Voice.   Enough! Enough! stop your singing!

Nandini [*sings on*].	*A lament heaves and bursts* *on the shore of the sea,* *The whispers of forgotten days* *are born in new leaves to die* *again.* See, Bishu, he has left the dead frog there and disappeared. He is afraid of songs.
Bishu.	The old frog in his heart yearns to die when it hears singing, that's why he feels afraid. My mad girl, why is there a strange light on your face to-day, like the glow of a distant torch in the sky?
Nandini.	News has reached me, Ranjan is coming to-day.
Bishu.	How?
Nandini.	Let me tell you. Every day a pair of blue-throats come and sit on the pomegranate tree in front of my window. Every night, before I sleep, I salute the pole star and say: Sacred star of constancy, if a feather

from the wings of the blue-throats finds its way into my room, then I will know my Ranjan is coming. This morning, as soon as I woke, I found a feather on my bed. See, here it is under my breast-cloth. When I meet him I shall put this feather on his crest.

Bishu.   They say blue-throats' wings are an omen of victory.

Nandini.   Ranjan's way to victory lies through my heart.

Bishu.   No more of this; let me go to my work.

Nandini.   I shan't let you work to-day.

Bishu.   What must I do then.

Nandini.   Sing that song of waiting.

Bishu [sings]. *He who ever wants me through the ages,—*

is it not he who sits to-day by my

> *wayside?*
> *I seem to remember a glimpse I had of*
> *his face,*
> *in the twilight dusk of some ancient*
> *year.*
> *Is it not he who sits to-day by the*
> *wayside?*

Nandini. Bishu, when you sing I cannot help feeling that I owe you much, but have never given anything to you.

Bishu. I shall decorate my forehead with the mark of your never- giving, and go my way. No little-giving for me, in return for my song! Where will you go now?

Nandini. To the wayside by which Ranjan is coming.

[*They go.*]

The Governor *and a* Headman *come in.*

Governor. No, we can't possibly allow Ranjan to enter this parish.

Headman.	I put him to work in the tunnels of Vajragarh.
Governor.	Well, what happened?
Headman.	He said he was not used to being made to work. The Headman of Vajragarh came with the police, but the fellow doesn't know what fear is. Threaten him, he bursts out laughing. Asked why he laughs, he says solemnity is the mask of stupidity and he has come to take it off.
Governor.	Did you set him to work with the diggers?
Headman.	I did, I thought that pressure would make him yield. But on the contrary it seemed to lift the pressure from the diggers' minds also. He cheered them up, and asked them to have a digger's dance!
Governor.	Digger's dance! What on earth is that?
Headman.	Ranjan started singing. Where were they to

get drums?—they objected. Ranjan said, if there weren't any drums, there were spades enough. So they began keeping time with the spades, making a joke of their digging up of nuggets.

The Headman himself came over to reprimand them. 'What style of work is this?' he thundered.

'I have unbound the work,' said Ranjan. 'It won't have to be dragged out by main force any more, it will run along of itself, dancing.'

Governor.   The fellow is mad, I see.

Headman.   Hopelessly mad. 'Use your spade properly,' shouted I. 'Much better give me a guitar,' said he, smiling.

Governor.   But how did he manage to escape from Vajragarh and come up here?

Headman.   That I do not know. Nothing seems to fasten on to him. His boisterousness is infectious. The diggers are getting frisky.

Governor. Hallo, isn't that Ranjan himself,—going along the road, thrumming on an old guitar? Impudent rascal! He doesn't even care to hide.

Headman. Well, I never! Goodness alone knows how he broke through the wall!

Governor. Go and seize him instantly! He must not meet Nandini in this parish, for anything.

Enters Assistant Governor.

Governor. Where are you going?

Assistant Governor. To arrest Ranjan.

Governor. Where is the Deputy Governor?

Assistant Governor. He is so much amused by this fellow that he doesn't want to lay hands on him. He says the man's laugh shows us what queer creatures we governors have grown into.

Governor.	I have an idea. Don't arrest Ranjan. Send him on to the King's sanctum.
Assistant Governor.	He refuses to obey our call, even in the King's name.
Governor.	Tell him the King has made a slave-girl of his Nandini.
Assistant Governor.	But if the King—
Governor.	Don't you worry. Come on, I'll go with you myself.

[*They go.*]

Enter **Professor** *and* **Antiquarian.**

Antiquarian	I say, what is this infernal noise going on inside?

Professor.   The King, probably in a temper with
                himself, is engaged in breaking some of
                his own handiwork.

Antiquarian   It sounds like big pillars crashing down
                one after another.

Professor.   There was a lake, at the foot of our hill over
                there, in which the waters of this Sankhini
                river used to gather. One day, suddenly, the
                rock to its left gave way, and the stored-up
                water rushed out laughing like mad. To
                see the King now-a-days, it strikes me that
                his treasure lake has grown weary of its
                rock wall.

Antiquarian. What did you bring me here for,
                Professor?

Professor.   Latterly he has begun to get angry with my
                science. He says it only burgles through
                one wall to reveal another behind it, and
                never reaches the inner chamber of the Life
                spirit. I thought that, perhaps in the study

of antiquity, he might explore the secret of Life's play. My knapsack has been rifled empty, now he can go on pocket-picking history.

Antiquarian.   A girl wearing a grass-green robe.

Professor.   She has for her mantle the green joy of the earth. That is our Nandini. In this Yaksha Town there are governors, foremen; headmen, tunnel-diggers, scholars like myself; there are policemen, executioners, and undertakers,—altogether a beautiful assortment! Only *she* is out of element. Midst the clamour of the market place she is a tuned-up lyre. There are days when the mesh of my studies is, torn by the sudden breeze of her passing by, and through that rent my attention flies away *swish*, like a bird.

Antiquarian.   Good heavens, man! Are even your well-seasoned bones subject to these poetic fits?

Professor. Life's attraction, like the tidal wave, tears away mind from its anchorage of books.

Antiquarian. Tell me, where am I to meet the King.

Professor. There's no means of meeting him. You'll have to talk to him from outside this network.

Antiquarian. We're to converse with this net between us?

Professor. Not the kind of whispered talk that may take place through a woman's veil, but solidly concentrated conversation. Even the cows in his stall don't dare to give milk, they yield their butter straight off!

Antiquarian. Admirable! To extract the essential from the diluted, is what scholars aim at.

Professor. But not what God in His creation aims at. He respects the fruit stones that are hard, but rejoices in the pulp that is sweet.

Antiquarian.   Professor, I see that your grey science is galloping fast towards grass-green. But I wonder how you can stand this King of yours.

Professor.   Shall I tell you the truth? I love him.

Antiquarian.   You don't mean to say so?

Professor.   He is so great that even what is wrong with him will not be able to spoil him.

The Governor *comes in.*

Governor.   I say, man of science, so this is the person you volunteered to bring here. Our King flew into a passion at the very mention of his special subject.

Antiquarian.   May I ask why?

Governor.   The King says there is no age of history which may be called old. It is always an eternal extension of the present,

Antiquarian.   Can the front exist without the back?

Governor.   What he said was: 'Time proceeds by
                  revealing the new on his front; but the
                  men of learning, suppressing that fact, will
                  have it that Time ever carries the burden of
                  the old on his back.'

Nandini *comes in hurriedly.*

Nandini.   What is happening? Who are they?

Governor.   Hallo, Nandini, is that you? I shall wear
                  your *kunda* chain late in the evening.
                  When three-quarters of me can hardly be
                  seen for the dark, then perchance a flower
                  garland might become even me.

Nandini.   Look over there-what a piteous sight! Who
                  are those people, going along with the
                  guards, filing out from the backdoor of the
                  King's apartments?

Governor.   We call them the King's leavings.

Nandini.   What does that mean?

Governor.   Some day you too will know its meaning;
         let it be for to-day.

Nandini.   But are these men? Have they flesh and
         marrow, life and soul?

Governor.   Maybe they haven't.

Nandini.   Had they never any?

Governor.   Maybe they had.

Nandini.   Where then is it all gone now?

Governor.   Man of science, explain it if you can, I'm off.

                                    [*He goes.*]

Nandini.   Alas, alas! I see amongst these shadows faces that I know. Surely that is our Anup and Upamanyu?

Professor.   They belong to our neighbouring village. Two brothers as tall as they were strong. They used to come and race their boats in our river on the fourteenth day of the moon in rainy June. Oh, who has brought them to this miserable plight? See, there goes Shaklu,—in sword play he used to win the prize garland before all the others. Anu-up! Sha-klu-u! look this way; it's I, your the principle underlying all rise to greatness.

Nandini.   It's a fiendish principle!

Professor.	It's no use getting annoyed with a principle. Principles are neither good nor bad. That which happens does happen. To go against it, is to knock your head against the law of being.
Nandini.	If this is the way of man's being, I refuse to be, I want to depart with those shadows,— show me the way.
Professor.	When the time comes for showing us out, the great ones themselves will point the way. Before that, there's no such nuisance as a way at all! You see how our Antiquarian has quietly slipped off, thinking he'll fly and save himself. After going a few steps, he'll soon discover that there's a wire.
Nandini [*knocking at the net window*].	Listen, listen!
Professor.	Whom are you calling?

Nandini.   That King of yours, shrouded in his mist
                    of netting.

Professor.   The door of the inner room has been
                    closed. He won't hear you.

Nandini   Bishu, mad brother mine!
[*calling out*].

Professor.   What d'you want with *him*?

Nandini.   Why hasn't he come back yet? I feel
                    afraid.

Professor.   He was with you only a little while ago.

Nandini.   The Governor said he was wanted to
                    identify Ranjan. I tried to go with him,
                    but they wouldn't let me. Whose groaning
                    is that?

Professor.   It must be that wrestler of ours.

Nandini.   What wrestler?

Professor.   The world-famous Gajju, whose brother, Bhajan, had the bravado to challenge the King to a wrestling match, since when not even a thread of his loin cloth is anywhere to be seen. That put Gajju on his mettle, and he came on with great sound and fury. I told him at the outset that, if he wanted to dig in the tunnels underneath this kingdom, he was welcome,—he could at least drag on a dead and alive existence for some time. But if he wanted to make a. show of heroics, that would not be tolerated for a moment.

Nandini.   Does it at all make for their well-being thus to keep watch and ward over these man-traps night and day?

Professor.   Well-being! There's no question of 'well' in it at all,— only 'being.' That *being* of theirs has expanded so terribly that, unless millions of men are pressed into service, who's going to support its weight? So the net is spreading farther and farther. They must exist, you see.

Nandini.

Must they? If it is necessary to die in order to live like men, what harm in dying?

Professor.

Again that anger, the wild cry of red oleander? It is sweet, no doubt, yet what is true is true. If it gives you pleasure to say that one must die to live, well, say so by all means; but those who say that others must die that. They themselves may live,—it's only they who are actually alive. You may cry out that this shows a lack of humanity, but you forget, in your indignation, that this is what humanity itself happens to be. The tiger does not feed on the tiger, it's only man who fattens on his fellow-man.

The Wrestler *totters in.*

Nandini.

Oh poor thing, see how he comes, staggering. Wrestler, lie down here. Professor, do see where he's hurt.

Professor.	You won't see any outward sign of a wound.
Wrestler.	All-merciful God, grant me strength once more in my life, if only for one little day!
Professor.	Why, my dear fellow?
Wrestler.	Just to wring that Governor's neck!
Professor.	What has the Governor done to you?
Wrestler.	It's he who brought about the whole thing. I never wanted to fight. Now, after egging me on, he goes about saying it's my fault.
Professor.	Why, what interest had he in your fighting?
Wrestler.	They only feel safe when they rob the whole world of strength. Lord of Mercy, grant that I may be able to gouge his eyes out some day, to tear asunder his lying tongue!

Nandini.	How do you feel now, Wrestler?
Wrestler.	Altogether hollowed out! These demons know the magic art of sucking away not only strength but hope. If only once I could somehow,—O good God, but once,—everything is possible to Thy mercy,—if only I could fasten my teeth for once in the Governor's throat!
Nandini.	Professor, help me to raise him.
Professor.	That would be a crime, Nandini, according to the custom of this land.
Nandini.	Wouldn't it be a crime to let the man perish?
Professor.	That which there is none to punish may be a sin, but never a crime. Nandini, come away, come right away out of this. The tree spreads its root-fingers and does its grabbing underground, but there it does not bring forth its flowers. Flowers bloom

on the branches which reach towards the light. My sweet Red Oleander, don't try to probe our secrets in the depths of their dust. Be for us swaying in the air above, that we may gaze upwards to see you.

There comes the Governor. He hates to see me talk to you. So I must go.

Nandini. Why is he so dead against me?

Professor. I can guess. You have touched his heart-strings. The longer it takes to tune them up, the more awful the discord meanwhile.

The Professor *goes, the* Governor *comes in.*

Nandini. Sir Governor!

Governor. Nandini, when our Gosain saw that *kunda* garland of yours in my room, both his eyes,—but here he comes—[*The Gosain comes in.*] Your Holiness, accept my reverence. That garland was given to me by our Nandini here.

Gosain.   Ah indeed! the gift of a pure heart! God's own white *kunda* flowers! Their beauty remains unsullied even in the hands of a man of the world. This is what gives one faith in the power of virtue, and hope for the sinners' redemption.

Nandini.   Please do something for this man, Your Reverence. There's very little life left in him.

Gosain.   The Governor is sure to keep him as much alive as it is necessary for him to be. But, my child, these discussions ill become your lips.

Nandini.   So in this kingdom you follow some calculation in apportioning life?

Gosain.   Of course,—for mortal life has its limits. Our class of people have their great burden to bear, therefore we have to claim a larger portion of life's sustenance for our share. That's according to almighty God's own decree.

Nandini.	Reverend Sir, may I know what good God has so heavily charged you to do to these people?
Gosain.	The life that is unlimited—gives no provocation to fight for its distribution. We Preachers have the charge of turning these people towards this unlimited life. So long as they remain content with that, we are their friends.
Nandini.	Let me come over to the Headman's quarters to help you.
Wrestler.	No. Don't add to my troubles, I beg of you. [*The* Wrestler *goes.*]
Nandini.	Governor, stay, tell me, whither have you taken my Bishu?
Governor.	Who am I that I should take him? The wind carries off the clouds,—if you think that to be a crime, make enquiries as to who is behind the wind.

Nandini.	Dear me, what an awful place! You are not men, and those you drive are not men, either,—you are winds and they are clouds! Reverend Gosain, I am sure, *you* know where my Bishu is.
Gosain.	I know, for sure, that wherever he is, it's for the best.
Nandini.	For whose best?
Gosain.	That you won't understand— Oh, I say, leave off, let go of that, it's my rosary.—Hallo, Governor, what wild girl is this you have—
Governor.	The girl has somehow managed to ensconce herself in a niche, safe from the laws of this land, and we can't lay hands on her. Our King himself—
Gosain.	Good heavens, now she'll tear off my wrap of the Holy Name too. What unspeakable outrage!

[*The* Gosain *flies.*]

Nandini.	Governor, you *must* tell me where you have taken Bishu.
Governor.	They have summoned him to the court of judgement. That's all that there is to tell you. Let me go.
Nandini.	Because I am a woman, you are not afraid of me? God sends His thunderbolt through His messenger, the lightning spark—that bolt I have borne here with me; it will shatter the golden spire of your mastery.
Governor.	Then let me tell you the truth before I go. It's you who have dragged Bishu into danger.
Nandini.	I?
Governor.	Yes, you! He was so long content to be quietly burrowing away underground like a worm. It's you who taught him to spread the wings of death. O fire of the gods, you'll yet draw forth many more to

their fate.—Then at length will you and I come to our understanding, and that won't be long.

Nandini.   So may it be. But tell me one thing before you go. Will you not let Ranjan come and see me?

Governor.   No, never.

Nandini.   Never, you say! I defy you to do your worst. This very day I am sure, absolutely sure, that he and I will meet!

                         [Governor *goes.*]

Nandini   Listen, listen, King! Where's your court
[*knocking and* of judgement? Open its door to me.
tugging at the   [*Kishor comes in.*]
network].   Who is that? My boy, Kishor! Do you know where Bishu is?

Kishor.   Yes, Nandini, be ready to see him. I don't know how it was, the Chief of the Guard took a fancy to my youthfulness and yielded to my entreaties. He has consented to take him along by this path.

Nandini.	Guard! Take him along? Is he then—
Kishor.	Yes; here they come.
Nandini.	What! Handcuffs on your wrists? Friend of my heart, where are they taking you like that?

Bishu *comes in under arrest.*

Bishu.	It's nothing to be anxious about!—Guards, please wait a little, let me say a few words to her.—My wild girl, my heart's joy, at last I am free.

Nandini.   What do you mean, Singer of my heart? I don't understand your words.

Bishu.   When I used to be afraid, and try to avoid danger at every step, I seemed to be at liberty; but that liberty was the worst form of bondage.

Nandini.   What offence have you committed that they should take you away thus?

Bishu.   I spoke out the truth to-day, at last.

Nandini.   What if you did?

Bishu.   No harm at all!

Nandini.   Then why did they bind you like this?

Bishu.   What harm in that either? These chains will bear witness to the truth of my freedom.

Nandini.   Don't they feel ashamed of themselves to lead you along the road chained like a beast? Aren't they men too?

Bishu. They have a big beast inside them, that's why their heads are not lowered by the indignity of man, rather the inner brute's tail swells and wags with pride at man's downfall.

Nandini. O dear heart! Have they been hurting you? What are these marks on your body?

Bishu. They have whipped me, with the whips they use for their dogs. The string of that whip is made with the same thread which goes to the stringing of their Gosain's rosary. When they tell their beads they don't remember that; but probably their God is aware of it.

Nandini. Let them bind me like that too, and take me away with you, my heart's joy! Unless I share some of your punishment I shan't be able to touch food from to-day.

Kishor.	I'm sure I can persuade them to take me in exchange for you. Let me take your place, Bishu.
Bishu.	Don't be silly!
Kishor.	Punishment won't hurt me. I am young. I shall bear it with joy.
Nandini.	No, no, do not talk like that.
Kishor.	Nandini, my absence has been noticed, their bloodhounds are after me. Allow me to escape the indignity awaiting me by taking shelter in a punishment I joyfully accept.
Bishu.	No, it won't do for you to be caught—not for a while yet. There's work for you, dear boy, and dangerous work too. Ranjan has come. You must find him out.
Kishor.	Then I bid you farewell, Nandini. What is your message when I meet Ranjan?

Nandini.	This tassel of red oleanders. [*Hands it to him.*]
	[Kishor *goes.*]
Bishu.	May you both be united once again.
Nandini.	That union will give me no pleasure now. I shall never be able to forget that I sent you away empty-handed. And what has that poor boy, Kishor, got from me?
Bishu.	Ail the treasure hidden in his heart has been revealed to him by the fire you have lighted in his life. Nandini, I remind you, it's for you to put that blue-throat's feather on Ranjan's crest.—There, do you hear them singing the harvest song?
Nandini.	I do, and it wrings my heart, to tears.
Bishu.	The play of the fields is ended now, and the field-master is taking the ripe corn home. Come on, Guards, let's not linger any more. [*Sings.*]

> *Mow the corn of the last*
> *harvest,*
> *bind it in sheaves.*
> *The remainder, let it return*
> *as dust unto the dust.*

[*They go.*]

The Governor and a Doctor come in.

Doctor.   I've seen him. I find the King.

Governor.   My wife will be driving out to-day. The
             post will be changed near your village, and
             you must see that she's not detained.

Headman.   There's a plague on the cattle of our parish,
             and not a single ox can be had to draw the
             car. Never mind, we can press the diggers
             into service.

Governor.   You know where you have to take her? To
             the garden-house, where the feast of the
             Flag-worship is to be held.

Headman.	I'll see to it at once, but let me tell you one thing before I go. That 69 Ng, whom they call mad Bishu,—it's high time to cure his madness.
Governor.	Why, how does he annoy you?
Headman.	Not so much by what he says or does, as by what he implies.
Governor.	There's no need to worry about him any further. You understand!
Headman.	Really! That's good news, indeed! Another thing. That 47 V, he's rather too friendly with 69 Ng.
Governor.	I have observed that.
Headman.	Your Lordship's observation is ever keen. Only, as you have to keep an eye on so many things, one or two may perchance escape your notice. For instance, there's our No. 95, a distant connection of mine

by marriage, ever ready to make sandals for the feet of Your Lordship's sweeper out of his own ribs,—so irrepressibly loyal is he that even his wife hangs her head for very shame,—and yet up to now—

Governor. His name has been entered in the High Register.

Headman. Ah, then his lifelong service will at last receive its reward! The news must be broken to him gently, because he gets epileptic fits, and supposing suddenly—

Governor. All right, we'll see to that. Now be off, there's no time.

Headman. Just a word about another person,—though he's my own brother-in-law. When his mother died, my wife brought him up with her own hands; yet for my master's sake—

Governor. You can tell me about him another time. Run away now.

Headman. There comes His Honour the Deputy Governor. Please speak a word to him on my behalf. He doesn't look upon me with favour. I suspect that when 69 Ng used to enjoy the favour of free entry into the palace, he must have been saying things against me.

Governor. I assure you, he never even mentioned your name.

Headman. That's just his cleverness! What can be more damaging than to suppress the name of a man, whose name is his best asset? These schemers have their different ways. No. 33 of our parish has an incurable a bit of haunting Your Lordship's private chamber. One is always afraid of his inventing goodness knows what calumnies about other people. And yet if one knew the truth about his own—

Governor.   There's positively no time to-day. Get
              away with you, quick!

Headman.   I make my salute. [*Coming back.*] Just
              one word more lest I forget. No. 88 of our
              neighbouring parish started work on a
              miserable pittance, and before two years
              are out his income has run into thousands,
              not to speak of extras! Your Lordship's
              mind is like that of the gods—a few words
              of hypocritical praise are enough to draw
              down the best of your boons.

Governor.   All right, all right,—that can keep for to-morrow.

Headman.   I'm not so mean as to suggest taking
              away the bread from his mouth. But Your
              Lordship should seriously consider whether
              it's wise to keep him on at the Treasury.
              Our Vishnu Dutt knows him inside out.
              If you send—

Governor.   I shall send for him this very day. But
              begone,—not another word!

Headman.	Your Lordship, my third son is getting to be quite a big boy. He came the other day to prostrate himself at your feet. After two days of dancing attendance outside, he had to go away without gaining admission to you. He feels it very bitterly. My daughter-in-law has made with her own hands an offering of sweet pumpkin for Your Lordship—
Governor.	Oh confound you! Tell him to come day after to-morrow, he will be admitted. Now, will you—

Headman *goes*. The Deputy Governor *comes in*.

Deputy Governor.	I've just sent on the dancing girls and musicians to the garden.
Governor.	And that little matter about Ranjan,— how far—?
Deputy Governor.	That kind of work is not in my line. The Assistant Governor has taken it

upon himself to do the job. By this time his—

Governor.   Does the King—?

Deputy   The King can't possibly have understood.
Governor.   Some lie told by our men has goaded
                 Ranjan to frenzy, and he's rushing to the
                 usual fate of—I detest the whole business.
                 Moreover, I don't think it right to deceive
                 the King like this.

Governor.   That responsibility is mine. Now then, that
                 girl must be—

Deputy   Don't talk of all that to me. The Headman
Governor.   who has been put on duty is the right man,—
                 he doesn't stick at any dirtiness whatever.

Governor.   Does that man Gosain know about this
                 affair?

Deputy   I'm sure he can guess, but he's careful not
Governor.   to know for certain.

Governor.	What's his object?
Deputy Governor.	For fear of there being no way left open for saying: 'I don't believe it.'
Governor.	But what makes him take all this trouble?
Deputy Governor.	Don't you see? The poor man is really two in one, clumsily joined,—Priest on the skin, Governor at the marrow. He has to take precious care to prevent the Governor part of him coming up to the surface, lest it should clash too much with his telling of beads.
Governor.	He might have dropped the beads altogether.
Deputy Governor.	No, for whatever his blood may be, his mind, in a sense, is really pious. If only he can tell his beads in his temple, and revel in slave-driving in his dreams, he feels happy. But for him, the true complexion of our God would appear too black. In fact,

Gosain is placed here only to help our God
to feel comfortable.

Governor.   My friend, I see the instinct of the Ruler
doesn't seem to match with the colour of
your own blood, either!

Deputy   There's hope still. Human blood is fast
Governor.   drying up. But I can't stomach your No.
321 yet. When I'm obliged to embrace
him in public, no holy water seems able to
wash out the impurity of his touch. Here
comes Nandini.

Governor.   Come away, I don't trust you. I know
the spell of Nandini has fallen on
your eyes.

Deputy   I know that as well as you do. But you don't
Governor.   seem to know that a tinge of her oleanders
has got mixed with the colour of duty in
your eyes too—that's what makes them so
frightfully red.

Governor.	That may be. Fortunately for us, our mind knows not its own secret. Come away. *[They go.]*

Nandini *comes in.*

Nandini [*knocking and pushing at the network*].	Listen, listen, listen!

The **Gosain** *comes in.*

Gosain.	Whom are you prodding like that?
Nandini.	That boa-constrictor of yours, who remains in hiding and swallows men.
Gosain.	Lord, lord! When Providence wishes to destroy the small, it does so by putting big words into their little mouths. See here, Nandini, believe me when I tell you that I aim at your welfare.

Nandini.	Try some more real method of doing me good.
Gosain.	Come to my sanctuary, let me chant you the Holy Name for a while.
Nandini.	What have I to do with the name?
Gosain.	You will gain peace of mind.
Nandini.	Shame, shame on me if I do! I shall sit and wait here at the door.
Gosain.	You have more faith in men than in God?
Nandini.	Your God of the Flagstaff,—he will never unbend. But the man who is lost to sight behind the netting, will he also remain bound in his network forever? Go, go. It's your trade to delude men with words, after filching away their lives.

[*The Gosain goes.*]

Enter Phagulal *and* Chandra.

Phagulal.	Our Bishu came away with you, where is he now? Tell us the truth.
Nandini.	He has been made prisoner and taken away.
Chandra.	You witch, you must have given information against him. You are their spy.
Nandini.	You don't really believe that!
Chandra.	What else are you doing here?
Phagulal.	Every person suspects every other person in this cursed place. Yet I have always trusted you, Nandini. In my heart I used to—However, let that pass. But to-day it looks very very strange, I must say.
Nandini.	Perhaps it does. It may really be even as you say. Bishu has got into trouble for coming with me. He used to be quite safe in your company, he said so himself.

Chandra.	Then why did you decoy him away, you evil-omened creature?
Nandini.	Because he said he wanted to be free.
Chandra.	A precious kind of freedom you have given him!
Nandini.	I could not understand all that he said. Chandra. Why did he tell me that freedom could only be found by plunging down to the bottom of danger?—Phagulal, how could I save him who wanted to be free from the tyranny of safety?
Chandra.	We don't understand all this. If you can't bring him back, you'll have to pay for it. I'm not to be taken in by that coquettish prettiness of yours.
Phagulal.	What's the use of idle bickering? Let's gather a big crowd from the workmen's lines, and then go and smash the prison gate.

Nandini.   I'll come with you.

Phagulal.   What for?

Nandini.   To join in the breaking.

Chandra.   As if you haven't done quite enough breaking already, you sorceress!

Gokul *comes in.*

Gokul.   That witch must be burnt alive, before everything else.

Chandra.   That won't be punishment enough. First knock off that beauty of hers, with which she goes about ruining people. Weed it out of her face as the grass is weeded with a hoe.

Gokul.   That I can do. Let this hammer just have a dance on her nose tip—

Phagulal.   Beware! If you dare touch her—

Nandini.   Stop, Phagulal. He's coward; he wants to strike me because he's afraid of me. I don't fear his blows one bit.

Gokul.   Phagulal, you haven't come to your senses yet. You think the Governor alone is your enemy. Well, I admire a straightforward enemy. But that sweet-mouthed beauty of yours—

Nandini.   Ah, so you too admire the Governor, as the mud beneath his feet admires the soles of his shoes!

Phagulal.   Gokul, the time has at length come to show your prowess, but not by fighting a girl. Come along with me. I'll show you what to fight.

                  [Phagulal, Chandra, *and* Gokul *go.*]

A band of men *come in.*

Nandini.   Where are you going, my good men?

First Man.	We carry the offering for the Flag-worship.
Nandini.	Have you seen Ranjan?
Second Man.	I saw him once, five days ago, but not since. Ask those others who follow us.
Nandini.	Who are they?
Third Man.	They are bearing wine for the Governors' feast.

[*The first batch goes, another comes in.*]

Nandini.	Look here, red-caps, have you seen Ranjan?
First Man.	I saw him the other day at the house of Headman Sambhu.
Nandini.	Where is he now?
Second Man.	D'you see those men taking the ladies' dresses for the feast? Ask them. They hear

a lot of things that don't reach our ears.

[*Second batch goes, a third come in.*]

Nandini.   Do *you* know, my men, where they have kept Ranjan?

First Man.   Hush, hush!

Nandini.   I am sure you know. You must tell me.

Second Man. What enters by our ears doesn't come out by our mouths, that's why we are still alive. Ask one of the men who are carrying the weapons.

[*They go, others come in.*]

Nandini.   Oh do stop a moment and listen to me. Tell me, where is Ranjan?

First Man.   The auspicious hour draws near. It's time for the King himself to come for the Flag-worship. Ask him about it when he steps out. We only know the beginning, not the end.   [*They go.*]

Nandini
[*shaking the
network
violently*].

Open the door. The time has come.

Voice [*behind
the scenes*].

But not for you. Go away from here.

Nandini.

You must hear *now* what I have to say. It cannot wait for another time.

Voice.

You want Ranjan, I know. I have asked the Governor to fetch him at once. But don't remain standing at the door when I come out for the worship, for then you'll run great risk.

Nandini.

I have cast away all fear. You can't drive me away. Happen what may, I'm not going to move till your door is opened.

Voice.

To-day's for the Flag-worship. Don't distract my mind. Get away from my door.

Nandini.	The gods have all eternity for their worship, they're not pressed for time. But the sorrows of men cannot wait.
King.	Deceived! These traitors have deceived me,—perdition take them! My own machine refuses my sway! Call the Governor— bring him to me handcuffed—
Nandini.	King, they all say you know magic. Make him wake up for my sake.
King.	My magic can only put an end to waking.— Alas! I know not how to awaken.
Nandini.	Then lull me to sleep,—the same sleep! Oh, why did you work this havoc? I cannot bear it any more.
King.	I have killed youth. Yes, I have indeed killed youth,—all these years, with all my strength. The curse of youth, dead, is upon me.
Nandini.	Did he not take my name?

King.   He did,—in such a way that every vein in
                my body was set on fire.

Nandini   My love, my brave one, here do I place
[to Ranjan].   this blue-throat's feather in your crest.
                Your victory has begun from to-day, and
                I am its bearer. Ah, here is that tassel of
                my flowers in his hand. Then Kishor must
                have met him— But where is he? King,
                where is that boy?

King.   Which boy?

Nandini.   The boy who brought these flowers to
                Ranjan. King. That absurd little child! He
                came to defy me with his girlish face.

Nandini.   And then? Tell me! Quick!
King.   He   burst   himself   against   me,
                like a bubble.

Nandini.   King, the Time is indeed now come!

King.   Time for what?

Nandini.   For the last fight between you and me.

King.   But I can kill you in no time,—this
                  instant.

Nandini.   From that very instant that death of
                  mine will go on killing you every single
                  moment.

King.   Be brave, Nandini, trust me. Make me
                  your comrade to-day.

Nandini.   What would you have me do?

King.   To fight against me, but with your hand in
                  mine. That fight has already begun. There is
                  my flag. First I break the Flagstaff,— thus!
                  Next it's for you to tear its banner. Let your
                  hand unite with mine to kill me, utterly
                  kill me. That will be my emancipation.

Guards   What are you doing, King? You dare
[rushing up].   break the Flagstaff, the holiest symbol of
                  our divinity? The Flagstaff which has its

one point piercing the heart of the earth and the other that of heaven! What a terrible sin,—on the very day of the Flag-worship! Comrades, let us go and inform our Governors. [*They run off.*]

King. A great deal of breaking remains to be done. You will come with me, Nandini?

Nandini. I will.

Phagulal *comes in.*

Phagulal. They won't hear of letting Bishu off. I am afraid, they'll—Who is this? The King! Oh you wicked witch,—conspiring with the King himself!
O vile deceiver!

King. What is the matter with you? What is that crowd out for?

Phagulal. To break the prison gate. We may lose our lives, but we shan't fall back.

King.   Why should you fall back? I too am out for breaking. Behold the first sign—my broken Flagstaff!

Phagulal.   What! This is altogether beyond us simple folk.
                 Be merciful, Nandini, don't deceive me. Am I to believe my eyes?

Nandini.   Brother, you have set out to win death. You have left no chance for deception to touch you.

Phagulal.	You too come along with. us, our own Nandini!
Nandini.	That is what I'm still alive for, Phagulal, I wanted to bring my Ranjan amongst you. Look there, he has come, my hero, braving death!
Phagulal.	Oh, horror! Is that Ranjan lying there, silent?
Nandini.	Not silent. He leaves behind him in death his conquering call. He will live again, he cannot die.
Phagulal..	Ah, my Nandini, my beautiful one, was it for this you were waiting all these eager days?
Nandini.	I *did* await his coming, and he *did* come. I still wait to prepare for his coming again, and he *shall* come again. Where is Chandra?

Phagulal.	She has gone with her tears and prayers to the Governor, accompanied by Gokul. I'm afraid Gokul is seeking to take up service with the Governor. He will betray us. King, are you sure you don't mistake us? We are out to break your own prison, I tell you!
King.	Yes, it is my *own* prison. You and I must work together, for you cannot break it alone.
Phagulal.	As soon as the Governor hears of it, he will march with all his forces to prevent us.
King.	Yes, my fight is against them.
Phagulal.	But the soldiers will not obey you.
King.	*You* will be on my side!
Phagulal.	Shall we be able to win through?
King.	We shall at least be able to die! At last

I have found the meaning of death. I am saved!

Phagulal. King, do you hear the tumult?

King. There comes the Governor with his troops. How could he be so quick about it? He must have been prepared beforehand. They have used my own power against me.

Phagulal. My men have not yet turned up.

King. They will never come. The Governor is sure to get round them.

Nandini. I had my last hope that they would bring my Bishu to me. Will that never be?

King. No hope of that, I'm afraid.

Phagulal. Then come along, Nandini, let us take you to a safe place first. The Governor will see red, if he but catches sight of you.

Nandini.	You want to banish me into the solitary exile of safety? [*Calling out*] Governor! Governor!—He has swung up my garland of *kunda* flowers on his spear-head. I will dye that garland the colour of my oleanders with my heart's blood.—Governor! He has seen me! Victory to Ranjan! [*Runs off.*]

King [*calling after her.*].   Nandini!

The Professor *comes in.*

Phagulal.   Where are you hurrying to, Professor?

Professor.   Some one said that the King has at last had tidings of the secret of Life, and has gone off in quest of it. I have thrown away my books to follow him.

Phagulal.   The King has just gone off to his death. He has heard Nandini's call.

Professor.   The network is torn to shreds! Where is Nandini?

Phagulal.	She has gone before them all. We can't reach her any more.
Professor.	It is only now that we shall reach her. She won't evade us any longer.

Professor *rushes out,* Bishu *comes in.*

Bishu.	Phagulal, where is Nandini?
Phagulal.	How did you get here?
Bishu.	Our workmen have broken into the prison. There they are,—running off to fight. I came to look for Nandini. Where is she?
Phagulal.	She has gone in advance of us all.
Bishu.	Where?
Phagulal.	To the last freedom. Bishu, do you see who is lying there?
Bishu.	Ranjan!

Phagulal.   You see the red streak?

Bishu.   I understand,—then red marriage.

Phagulal.   They are united.

Bishu.   Now it is for me to take my last journey.—
                Perhaps we may meet.—Perhaps she
                may want me to sing.—My mad girl,
                O my mad girl!—Come, brother, on
                to the fight!

Phagulal.   To the fight! Victory to Nandini!

Bishu.   Victory to Nandini!

Phagulal.   Here is her wristlet of red oleanders.
                She has bared her arm to-day,—and
                left us.

Bishu.   Once I told her I would not take anything
                from her hand. I break my word and take
                this. Come along!

                                              [*They go.*]

Song in the distance.
Hark 'tis Autumn calling,—
Come, O come away!
The earth's mantle of dust is filled with
ripe corn!
O the joy! the joy!

Other Classics in the Tagore Series

- The King of the Dark Chamber

- Fire Flies

- Fruit Gathering

- Gitanjali

- Malini

- Nationalism

- Religion of man

- Sacrifice

- The Crescent Moon

- The Crown

- The Fugitive